Confidence

Sundress Publications • Knoxville, TN

Copyright © 2015 by Sandra Marchetti
ISBN: 978-1-939675-16-3
Published by Sundress Publications

Editor: Erin Elizabeth Smith
erin@sundresspublications.com
http://www.sundresspublications.com

Colophon: This book is set in Goudy Old Style

Cover Design: Brian Mihok

Cover Image: Jan Van Huysum

Book Design: Erin Elizabeth Smith and Marika von Zellen

Confluence
Sandra Marchetti

Danielle,
   Thank you so
much for organizing
such a fabulous event —
one I will _never_ forget!
With appreciation for
you fine poems,
   ~ S

Sandra Marchetti

My deep gratitude to Eric Pankey, Sally Keith, Andrew Hudgins, Harryette Mullen, and Scott Semple, for giving their eyes and ears to this work.

I would also like to thank the Vermont Studio Center for affording me time and space to complete this project during the summer of 2013.

For Scott, my most generous reader.

Contents

It is like what we imagine knowledge to be:
dark, salt, clear, moving, utterly free,
drawn from the cold hard mouth
of the world, derived from the rocky breasts
forever, flowing and drawn, and since
our knowledge is historical, flowing, and flown.

~Elizabeth Bishop, from "At the Fishhouses"

Never-Ending Birds

Soft bulbs of morpho blue,
tight light pruned to a circuit,
the swallows feather and vector the wind.

I plume to watch, freshed in the ground;
they ring the trees as their own
sweet planets. Continuous streaks,
the green-blue preens take flying lessons,

beam to the ground they are bound by,
like no flown thing. They bring
around the ground and bright as floods
in winter, flap the wind that takes them,

pushes them into its envelope. The swallows,
so close, beat; I let them scrim
my stance, twist neatly solar.

I swallow, lift at my chest where the freckles
crack, where the wet wings gleam. Swallows
sweep out to swing my heart up with the hawk
who circles the skirmish, weeps, and screams.

Sur l'herbe

You miss it, craning
away from verdancy.

Pause in this place
while I glaze you;
my head tilts
a direction you can't read.

Green leaves drape
a frame of velvet.

Don't move:
you can't see
you are a strange
portrait.

Like Manet,
I strain each stroke
of cup and nape
to show I can,

then muddle you
toward the boughs to sway
in wilderness already named.

The Return

"figurations of mist
at the turn of the corner,
figurations of time
at the bend in this pause,"
~*Octavio Paz, trans. Eliot Weinberger*

Beyond the body itself
is the thin blue line,
the sky folding back on its spine.

I saw today the paper gold mists,
the terrible last burnings off of morning;

I have an idea that you ate me then,
and slid belching through the fog—

you slicked my breast
on past your teeth and tasted
my unsalted skin.

I'm small; I know when I've been
swallowed whole, been rounded out
gold and beaming,

become a curve in your smile,
the element of light—broken on the tide—
the start of day.

Island Park

*According to local legend, in the last century numerous
suicide attempts have taken place off the railroad bridge in
this Geneva, Illinois park.*

We chased
the heron, the bridge,
a rafting concrete wave
hefted high.

My jaw dredged across
the watery flood blood—
green water and open
to receive me off

the bastion train track,
bust track—
a human's perch,
a faction, a fraction—

to be untied,
and given to granite,
carved into a willing water.
A dressage of slipping rocks
braced for the fall.

Fleshed against
the sidewalls
of underwater
blood canyons,

our flexed stomachs carve
cold tidal eaves,
shredding skin,
making shifts of ice.

What's young
comes lick-swift, dying
quick off the two-tiered bridge.
A loud past flinches
the nuclear edges.

Water lilies and
still-motioning swings:
this is the heron's
pick-ground.

Peninsula

A washed ring of sounds,
rocks glazed with boat music.
Clouds soot the forests in delicate black salt.

A dead fish—bass or bluegill—
is half-gone back to the rocks and beyond,
lies no-eyed on the shoreline.

Its extant others—us in canoes and kayaks—
merge to the white strait horizon
and wish to reach up—

flexed fingers grab canopy,
chill-cliffs, a dark-formed maze.

I am seven times the size and climbing—
slamming my cheeks into birches,
moving north through the dark day.

Storm Dialogue

Storms turn on their stomachs and gain on us.
Cloud decks smoke the windows. Beating cold.

Rain comes in shifts and pisses. Moving west
is the gesture; the skies shave the city gray.

The eastern sky is filled hammocks,
storms twin up like rough moons rising.

Off over our minds,
over the tips of our touch,

razed fields of air click
their wet fingers, hit the glass and ride.

Blue-Black

Sweat rains
over a river—
I stir in you,
delight in
our slick.

We rub our eyes until
we've made owls
of each other:
under the lurching
fur of eyebrows,
the blue and green
of our sight glows,
flicks out and open.

I pull my body,
an alabaster mask,
and push—your fingers
like pale spires
against me.

Here in the night of it,
an hour where dark weaves
between the trees' trunks,
the black hooves
of the earth,

we release names.
We become studies
in identity,
lasting until you
sleep to sense.

Awake,
I am ethereal against you.
I come into the curve,
I lay down the other—
light uncurls from foreign hands.

Silver

Wheel and lock,
your irises drop
into mine and sink.
My skin a new bird,
white in the morning-bright
and newly downy.

Hands against
a shoulder scrape,
then release between
an arm and under.
I pull up toward
your eye;

the triangles of our bodies
lie, then slide.
A light writes out
from us and dies
where we cut
our shadow.

Oh hum me to a crest,
so we buzz with each
other's blood:
a cicada's clean song
of shedding.

Lunch

After a two-mile walk to the stand,
I open a spigot on the raspberries—
blush hearts in the hand.

The crackers brick against my lips,
slide through a stick of butter;
I rub dirt from the tomatoes.

Sorting the demands of red-orange,
pink, cream, I flick stems on the bank,
watch them wash downstream. It is noon,

the bees are circling for somewhere to land.
Fruit breaks on my teeth, spreads
through the mouth's star—a galaxy expands.

Autumn Damask

Come.
Let me show you
the blown open roses
of nearly November.

Geese land in a card deck shuffle.
Their fingers sweep the ground
then plait down the body.

Lie fetal on the ground.
In the Midwest you will see
the world split—
a lidded eye drawn open as if
by marionette leads.

The willows are four crowns pointing down.

Comfort is when
you are tethered
to a place
you couldn't move
fast from anyway.

Roam the ground where you are
mapped, flat and free, beneath
this sky, this new sea.

The Language of Ice

Crowns of birds emerge and sink,
skid to the river in blinking beats.
Jagged as glass, ice flashes match
memories of church windows, a glacial past.
Lines of a pencil afloat mark a bobbing post,
bags beneath drift, seek their currents like fish.

Twist—the tree calls us to see roots straight to meet
concrete then broke above like floes pulled up;
a stretching shrine, bark chases the water's
spine—a blind grasp toward glinting.

Branches reach behind their back,
trill the stream to sing
a glad racket of sounds that smack
of crowning winter's gleam.

"Cold dark deep and absolutely clear"
~Elizabeth Bishop

The water a sheet of beat tin, it is a June song
in March, ripples for welcome. Army and gray
colors tell us why the season resists the call

of our bodies; displayed on the nightstand, the interior
brave replica of summer, stilted
in daguerreotype, printed gauzily. The white light

needed over our shoulders to see the ream, the functioning
slide. The bed is yellow—a blushing pastel paper
out of context in the hoarfrost season. Even

the white bell doilies breathe in dust
from the half-light time. Not entirely shade
but clear gray out across the ledge

and many measures more, a little water flits
between a split-trunk tree. It is
what we imagine June to be: a sliver

of wet movement, an arc that asks for colors
to ice it hotly and shake the shake of gray.

Skyward

The moon resolves
to a crescent of sparrows;

their cloud snags
the telephone poles.

Beaks pass
the car's roof,

become a lone
jet headed west,

a transformation of loft.

The birds disappear—
they were never here—

a bait and switch
after which I point.

The East Highlands

*The East Highlands was the first subdivision built in
Naperville, Illinois, 30 miles outside of Chicago. The Moser
Lumber Company began construction shortly after World
War II.*

i. Dozer

You took me to my old neighborhood. You took me
to my old neighborhood and I recognized names. Cat,
Construction Experts, Building Company, Midwest Landscape.

You took me to my old neighborhood
and I recognized the trees I'd left behind merged
to one last. The birch gone. Yes, the one that looked
as if it was dying—well—not looking.

We went to my old neighborhood and even
the streetlights had switched places. Your lawn
was my lawn. My house in heaven, yours
crumbled to bits just below.

We went to my old neighborhood and I said
a prayer for the 1,000 square foot ranch,
the window unit air conditioner.
I read last rites to your raspberry patch.

You took me to our old neighborhood; the single
tree wept over my shoulder. Scraped me
with maple fingernails. Released its grip
on time. In my old neighborhood, the sun's poking

through time. Time's waking up before dawn.
Cat's about to eat through with steel mandibles.

ii. Memory: Wellner Road

Wellner—as in a hollowing out and then naming it,
a place slipped back behind something else: here,
another road named Sleight. Sleight and Wellner,
Wellner. It hollowed and dipped; a bike downstream could go at measureable winds.

I came from under the canopy,
the starched hammock, bounced off the sky
like a child's ball, and whipped past the drive's trees:
the neighborhood's invisibility.

In a car I rode up and back,
massaging the horizon's edge, looking
through the roof's opening, toward branchy
reachings. How they said, come.

The doze, the lull of Wellner, that nothing-of-noise,
nothing-of-note but beauty, then 'Sold' on its shoulders,
up the street. Who wanted to leave?
A man came quickly to survey.

I walked down to hear him say, "Prune back, landscape.
        Modern place?"
Then a swallowing chop. The interior play—
my mother at the television, my father across town—
but the cover creeping, the branches strayed
away from the canopy, the hole eaten in that sheet.

iii. Memory: Backyard

In the raspberry patch we looked for ones
that weren't green anymore. We rooted
under the pawing outgrowths. Next to
the raspberry bushes were poison berries.

My mother climbed in over me,
prickling as she knelt
and bent and threw back stalks
at the blue-veined center.

The raspberry patch, a shady semicircle
of seven feet, butted our neighbor's fence—
fat red slats with berries
and a dog on the opposite side.

We walked slung up with Tupperware,
novices growing for the twelfth spring.
We'd pack and freeze berries from the patch,
trip the plastic black around its edge. I'd fall
in the bushes and reel, knees to the grass.

The raspberries came back, almost
like in a novel, and when we went out, they laid
for us, little fussing hearts.

Borderland

What will happen now—
what now in the tallow,
low-tapped blind light,

under the shaded
blinds, beyond the canopy
of one fevered tree?

What will stir this pool later
when it closes up
blue and under sun?

Who is gnawing at your waters?
Setting his forked hands against you?

I wonder who it calls
on weekday evenings.
Old women walk around it,

their dogs bark and shake their stuff.
Fenced out, they riff in licks and bits
of chlorine, aching to bruise—but then—yield.

What are you?
A country.

Late Games

Bad egg moon—
Brie with a hard crust.

Not a rising, but a movie
across the shift of night.

Light games illuminate
the players of the dark:

the white and shadows of 40,000 fans
curled around a diamond beaming green,

the lovers' tilted lampshades
pushing angles of cream luminescence.

Ivoried city moon, the glory
of your yolk spills out,

rotten and dissolved,
running like a marathon nightlight.

Music

Soft being, your skin
grips slunked shoulders
and shut eyes, singed.

I cup your curve; you begin
to comport your nudeness,
sing breath into my face.

Between your thighs
is a cannon awake. I make
tracks against your skin in tangles;

retouching, our bodies
slink at accordion angles:
nose, arms, and knees.

I haul you into me,
running my palms
through the curves of your slack

breath like ashen water, salt sea.
Watch as I assemble you—
sing yourself asleep for me.

Migration Theory

The womb a tent,
lit from within, flutters
golden on the wind.

I'm given to pregnancy
dreams again.

Sleeping, the world becomes round once more—
sleeping atop my midriff. Sleeping in
silence and veins and skin—a globe, a missive.

I'm told the child
is ghost; instead

the sleep is lifted into,
alight with curiosities
curling out from the hand.

Sleep. The light sheet ruffles within.
White moths in flight
lift from the body—the skin.

Hollow

Cracking eggs open—
click into bowl,

bowl into yolk,
eye into eye,

I told that oven story,
how I forgot to light it,

then I finally lit up in it—
gas singeing

then a swallowing
crunch.

The fruit of my throat
constricted on the fruit

of the apple's skin,
the curled red

non-viscous wrap;
I laughed

and pushed myself
toward the sink.

Tried to take water—
to take your eyes on me—

the eggs in the bowl
already loosed, peeled,

the peel turning in me,
wet and covering.

I stopped,
lurched

and the red popped
out, choked chew,

with champagne meat
still inside.

You turned, gave
me water;

I coughed
and spoke low—

"Fine, fine; don't I
sound...?"

You glanced into
the eggs—

the glaze of the bowl,
the glaze

of viscous centers
existing.

"You finished cracking
them. You finished anyway."

Nodding, I wanted you
to believe I was a miracle,

as I believe you are
a miracle.

Afternoon Reading

The glinted day
flips open and falls.

Waiting and wanting
is how I read the morning;

my eyes book the hours
and watch words slip-swim

to the ears
of other writers' loves.

I hear them talk
and we are darkened
in the fleece of their pages.

The eye of the spine cracks
and then you are there—

I close the binding to look up,
turn but it's a jay—

widening his body
toward me, the stilting
beak laid down.

Spiral Orb

Atop the street, lamplights curl
like spider legs.

Cars shuttle web beams
slung through the sky.

Knit my astral eyes
in bleared light, through mirrors

I catch the northern star
in lit-up cars;

I near the northern drapery
and wave, uncurling.

Spindling legs charm us
from the road

toward the swaying spinnerets,
the slow dance light show.

Town

Town is a place we never knew before.
Walking by windows higher than us,
Tiffany lamps shine beside the corners of our eyes.

Light slides from the bookstore's bank of glass
and the shivering Christmas wires, lifting off their canopies,
impose new lumen on already bright trees.

Trees are shelved with books, too. Our gaze
layers and reverses through glass: a spice shop pressed
in brambles, jewelers' cases, a lit doorway.

Sidewalks fall into light, then gather dark pools.
Headlights and streetlights gleam the same Sirius
color, riding windows in stop-motion.

Inside the panes, where heat presses, we see
how crowded we've become: lights and drop
ceilings reach over stars and take territory.

Warm signs glow, reflected above the escalators.
The electric stairs move legs up the narrow street:
through lamplight and braking cars,
past the library toward the next sky.

Saints

How crowded
the stars become in your eye—
you dazzle with a miracle inside—
the Lady of Guadalupe, you are

so sweet and so cold,
impasto olive skin
and tears set in glass.

They say
a glass with water
is the very hardest thing

to paint, the light
reflecting, a globe suspended
in wet wonder.

The Dutch could do this—
hold water in their eyes—
inside the painter

a glass would become full,
a flower fresh
with drops of dew,
insects on the petals.

The Canopy

Recognize me unbudded,
in green-tinctured
powder puff pink:
a carnation's crumple.

Skirts and lumen sink
into sweet-sway hills,
brightened grasses.

Spare trees swell
on the greenway's
flattened escalator.

My eyes tighten, as the tongue
presses against the roof—
eyeing the sky in the dark
story

of the mouth—
which is smooth, fixed.
It unbolts. It says.

Crushed skirts knit the canopy—
become a canopy and finely rise.

Birds exchange trees in a mellow harmony.

I am not so free—not free but swelling—
and I sing in exchange of trees.

Places

I'm hoping one day to climb through my mind:
around donut-shaped crooks and a cavity-corridor,
to divide the world between those lobes.

I have always wanted to climb it,
for my toe to stick within the slipped loops
then grip again, like an octopus nearing coral

slipping its jointless arm around it and then
shrinking, shrinking into the sea.

Dillard says she can see columns of air, not
just the insects that live in them. I see the tiny
roses on my bed sheet—thousands—they might

as well be eggs of the octopus, or those holding
within the cargo sacs of the insects. I see
the roses sewn into foursquare and know

the brain can multiply, bring into being square
meters of light, or just a pattern that leads
back toward no edge.

A rose blooms and lowers its neck, slipping
its scents for the last time. Anxious in sleep,
I traverse each corner again.

I don't move: only the fingerless slips,
the soul ribbons past.

From Here

Click the day
and see suns rise—
my mind cracks up
with the blinds.

Rise in incremental shinings:
the glass light between
leaves and their shadows.

Click the day,
the wheel to turn
from here upon.

The river rises and I slide:
cautious to tell
when time shuts out.

Days shut upon days:
cracks, like in asphalt
slabs, are shored in place.

Click the day
with a counting clock,
a meter to measure
who's opened your door.

Slick one, see it gleam?
The shifting, rising
of morning's bread—

Swing

Trace a line, fine,
around the valley's run,

your hand rigid upon
the canopy's brown wool, spun.

Ridges—at length—are cardboard or lakes
hung high as mirrors.

Your heels click ahead
bound after a zephyr.

Ride your eye along the bank,
slide down the forested sky

to hear through songbirds' skittering
a coyote's chattered cry.

Divinity Redux

Do we see the face?
That origin flash
of what's human?

Is that what we do,
in the white bed,
in the white room
glowing clean?

~

From windows on the garden
we look out with our bodies

as they massage each other,
pulling the cream,
the thin liquids through.

Do we see the face
when the damp slips
from our twin suns?

We observe ourselves
enacting pure sex—
but it isn't that—

~

We meet in the face,
in the shallow sockets
where we lay,

and in their blinking task:
of stretching small fingers,

like withered tree branches,
through our minds,

converging in each
caverned hallway

to fire light
into our grins.

The Washing
for Scott

Curved like nautilus shells,
milk-white with golden ribbing,

our spines slope to the sink;
we bow over the warmed water.

I curl toward the basin,
as to pray, as to be cleaned.

The washrag fills and falls,
water slipping down your hands and mine.

You lift it to my face,
wring it out

and let the water run
against my chin, my neck.

Drying my eyes,
you dip the cloth back in

and take it for yourself,
hold it against your skin,

cool and wet, you sigh.

Girl in Stone

I'm sheaving off the morning
in swells and scrolls,

Athena's curls wave
past my back to the sea.

Diadems of light come forward
in sweet births. The day

laurels in their neat way
turn to greet me—

I slip my sandal up
the fluted curves, the steps

that roll over, Ionic,
stomped in place
like divots in a loaf.

My eyes, without irises,
gaze into place.

Round ovums, sleep centers—
they fall back to sockets, soft

as children come
to nest beneath my arms.

The Waters of Separation

Laugh with me here
on the faster side
of forever;

come to the river bright
from the cleaning bugs
and wait on this.

I motion out to you now;
the sun raises the ghosts
of particles in tiny half-life.

Come and keep this song;
in the daylight,
under broke clouds

torn twice through,
we wait riven
to the rocks peeling back,
black in the water.

I find you, my darling,
knelt down and stung
by the softness
by the smoked waters

across from where we are—
on the faster side
of the stream—now fleeting.

Storefront

Light in the wings,
down to the vein,

the honeybee's
plum and gold.

Near a windowsill,
the black bands dip

like rags slipped
in the fan's wheel.

Little wings spin,
sharp and bright,

points glinting in the sun
show smooth as blades at night.

Orange Bouquet

The cauliflower encourages shock—
a fat bulb you loosed

from the stalk, grown
all summer to give itself up.

The dark farm in diorama
crams between each branch.

I brush caterpillars into the sink
and geese wink out, smatter

dirt on my hands
in their landing.

Without a knife, each flower
clicks clean from the stem

as you said it would,
in a backward crack,

a snap of the head.

Run

Repeat to me
the rhythm of the drop.

Repeat and reap
a cold, ugly beat,

repeat the Rhône,
the bird coursing up

and in-between wire
and sheaving sweet rains.

Repeat the arrow
made by a rock

in the river's run,
repeat it, drop—

drop and sling,
repeat down the river

and see the green,
the brown light die

over the lawn chairs'
wet wood, pried.

Repeat to me
the mosquito's bite,

scan the willows
from the fish's sight.

The Curve

I think of the midriff,
that time between wound and healing,
summer and winter—

the midriff,
a woman's place,
smooth, round, anywhere.

Pale and bowed,
a bell or a pear,
it's always ready.

I think of transitions—
slipping-swift days,
where I lie furred as a moth

under a domed sky.
I sleep and wake,
eat an apple

and throw the core out,
just missing the bag
that lines the wastebasket.

I lie ruddy-faced and wild,
vigilant in rest, untested.
I imagine the dying willow grove,

dead only for six months,
as the moths
and the apple's core.

White scores the sky and blue interrupts.

The gray roses in ecstasy
run into winter,
point at my face, my knees.

Everywhere is sharp edges
even outside rooms.
I am attempting to see.

As hibernation begins in the world,
I find my first narrow gate
into the snow, the wild dead forests of winter.

A man runs with his dog
up a path toward the road.

I sweet here in my syrup,
and lie under the snow-lit skies,
soon to bring stars to the ground.

Pilgrims

A meteor slung
over the river thrums
the sky's drumhead.

The stream stitches itself,
a crosshatched quilt
lofted atop the bedrock.

Rivulets wisp the bank,
grind a heron's feet
into sand; prints

etch a place
where cells shut off,
one by living one.

Fissures

By night
my body disconnects, falls,

lies on the bed in bones
and curls of hair.

There is nothing
to join it.

Skin flicks off
through shudders, and furls—

I lay and am unhitched,
unrolled.

I see what is done darkly,
between shadows and the neatest black.

The low lake below
lets go its nets,

from joints I wash toward confluence,
dissolved in a room of night.

Grace

Lie flat on your back
in the black lake

this night of your
annunciation.

The water's still
until sprung,

lapping at your
body afloat.

You model suspension.
Over the bridge,

the flat black
moths rise,

circle the violet sky,
the sand, you at the center.

You lie still as
stared-at heaven.

Blank and enormous,
the moths flick off your face

and round the lake
in a night circus

until the dark wings alight,

twist your body
in cold twilight.

On the shoreline, a fawn stops midflight
and hops—shook toward night.

Tea

My breath skates
across the glass,
golden scales push off
in electric bright
rifles at dawn.

I sip the flowers.
They flesh
in a way I see
when deposed of you,
carefully.

Now is the time for silence
of recognition—
the wintering observation.
I am a centering figure
bright to catch.

The lit wick of you
sleeps in another country.
I look at the glass,
watch a flower unfurl
and darkly lit, I fall.

Pastoral

There is a foot on the ground, a caked and kicked up
foot and a half. I crunch my boots in for respite,
survey the scape where the year's poems
were written, harvested, baled up, when

the grass seemed preternaturally green and is
now a hiding, gnomish weed; even the tall grass
braces in the rightwise facing snow. Snow is

not white but blue at blue hour,
in dusky half-light. A snow machine's
owl-lit eye culls it into sanskrit
piles and mushes, parallel faces. The light

writes out from the woods and across
the baseball field afield, a watery diamond in Spring:
this is no late March day. The driver escapes
in figure eights and twists around the brown

willow diadems. I stand wrung up, by feet
fixed in their mush-spots; cold's tight arrow
plunges my chest. This is why I go out,
I think; it is something to recover from.

Wind freezes the skirts of white swaying
earthward. The let is in the house, a let up
in the house and not before. Last year
writhes in a heavy, snow-down blanket.

The poems are there, too:
loose-written in the tall grass,
hewn to a willowbend,
a path's end now before me.

Walk Through

I walk through our home in mind
to make a cup of coffee.
Greeting leaves in the picture window,
I seem slow to grind the beans.

A crystal dish—the things I love—
the rooms gleam white and clean.
Our desk is neat between
your bills, my calendar and pen,

the floor plan gauzed beyond a screen.
Be tidying when I come, dust me off—
another thing. I bring to you
The Late Romances, the walls suffuse in cream.

Our room, your face, the porcelain,
light unbuttons the dream.
I itch my eyes open to fix
on minnows squirting downstream.

By Degrees

Geese triangulate the sky,
beating toward the gramophones
of each other.

One slides from the isosceles
right to angle in the back fleet.
Lock-swift symmetry.

Move over and be as you should be.

A light's out in the library reading room.
Pleats of Western sky
meet in the gilt-dimmed dusk.

Move over and be. As you should be.

Lattice

I dreamt my ring
    dissolved last night
into bits of silver
    and diamond chips.

The antique stone
    swallowed somewhere,
taken from its case,
    my fingers, crushed to cracks.

In the morning I cut a mango,
    a weathered stone fruit,
and slip down the center,
    furling my knife away just as I hit.

I carve around the core; the orange
    crystal peels off like cake
layers flush to reveal the diamond,
    the white sculpted center
of the ring,
    the cut away day.

Vanishing Point

A strip of falls rises against its horizon.
Low in the leaves, my cry latches
to a cloud ribboning from view.

The tumblers in my eyes click
as you prune stems,
bind them to a pack.

From behind my mother's garage
I hand you a lily,
years past its creation.

One Secret

So not to miss the moment of you, I stay my gaze,
hit play on the slapdash shrieked recorder of now.
The blue table slides from under your pupil
and out toward mine—motions in sign—
the language reminds: we will know each
others' bodies now, know how they will change.

Dusk flares the bones' groan, so I rub your stomach
until you sleep. I neat my breath to yours,
as if you were a child; the confluence
of rhythms begins. It is only sound
and meaning. Sound and meaning.

Notes

"Never-Ending Birds" borrows its title from David Baker's poetry collection of the same name.

"Sur l'herbe" alludes to Édouard Manet's landmark modernist painting, "Le déjeuner sur l'herbe."

"The Return" is prefaced by a section of Octavio Paz's poem, "As one listens to the rain."

"Autumn Damask" employs the line, "...each rose completely blown open," from "Cloud Country" by Carl Phillips.

"'Cold dark deep and absolutely clear'" is titled after the refrain in Elizabeth Bishop's poem, "At the Fishhouses." A section of her poem also provides this book's epigraph.

"Migration Theory" owes something to the language of Robert Frost's "The Silken Tent."

"Saints" makes use of a line, "so sweet and so cold," from William Carlos Williams' "This Is Just To Say."

"Places" alludes to Annie Dillard's ability to "focus along that column of air, picking out flying insects," a skill she describes in her memoir, *Pilgrim at Tinker Creek.*

"Girl in Stone" borrows some imagery from Sylvia Plath's "Edge."

"The Waters of Separation" references the Biblical concept of a ceremonial cleansing after one has come into contact with the dead.

"Walk Through" makes mention of *The Late Romances*, a grouping of William Shakespeare's later plays, including *The Tempest* and *The Winter's Tale.*

Acknowledgments

I give my deep gratitude to the editors and staffs of the following publications, in which these poems—sometimes in different versions—previously appeared:

Atticus Review: "Skyward"
The Bakery: "Borderland," "The Canopy," "Migration Theory"
Blue Lyra Review: "The Language of Ice," "Swing"
Cider Press Review: "Storefront"
CURA: "Town"
dirtcakes: "Fissures"
Flycatcher: "Silver"
Flyway: "Orange Bouquet," "Pilgrims"
Gargoyle: "The Return"
Green Mountains Review: "Walk Through"
The Hollins Critic: "Lunch"
The Journal: "Blue-Black," "Hollow"
Menacing Hedge: "Spiral Orb," "The Waters of Separation,"
          "Vanishing Point"
Nashville Review; Subtropics: "Never-Ending Birds"
Phoebe: "'Cold dark deep and absolutely clear,'" "Island Park"
Poydras Review: "Peninsula"
Redactions: "Saints"
Rock & Sling: "By Degrees"
Spiral Orb: "Places"
Spurt Literary Journal: "The East Highlands"
Stirring: "Autumn Damask"
Stone Highway Review: "One Secret," "Lattice," "Music," "Tea"
Sugar House Review: "Girl in Stone"
Thrush Poetry Journal: "Sur l'herbe"
Tupelo Quarterly: "Grace"

Some of these poems also appear in a chapbook, *The Canopy*, published by Midwest Writing Center Press.

Additionally, *A Detail in the Landscape*, a fine print edition published by Eating Dog Press includes work from this collection.

Poems from *Confluence* are anthologized in *New Poetry from the Midwest*, *The World Is Charged: Poetic Engagements with Gerard Manley Hopkins*, and *Parts of the Whole: Poems of the Body*.

A few pieces have been featured or reprinted in The Wardrobe, *After Hours*, *Redux*, *Patria Letteratura*, and *Extract(s)*.

About the Author

Sandra Marchetti holds an MFA in Creative Writing-Poetry from George Mason University. In 2014, Eating Dog Press published a fine print illustrated edition of Sandy's essays and poetry, *A Detail in the Landscape*, and her first volume, *The Canopy*, won Midwest Writing Center's 2011 Mississippi Valley Chapbook Contest. Sandy won Second Prize in Prick of the Spindle's 2014 Poetry Open Competition and her work appears in *Blackbird*, *The Journal*, *Subtropics*, *The Hollins Critic*, *Sugar House Review*, *Mid-American Review*, *Thrush Poetry Journal*, *Green Mountains Review*, *South Dakota Review*, *Southwest Review*, *Phoebe*, *The Rumpus*, and elsewhere. She currently works as a writing instructor and creative manuscript editor outside of her native Chicago.

Other Sundress Publications Titles

Hallelujah for the Ghosties
Melanie Jordan
ISBN 978-1939675156
$12.00

Fortress
Kristina Marie Darling
ISBN 978-1939675132
$12.00

When I Wake It Will Be Forever
Virginia Smith Rice
ISBN 978-1939675101
$12.00

The Lost Animals
David Cazden
ISBN 978-1939675071
$12.00

A House of Many Windows
Donna Vorreyer
ISBN 978-1939675057
$12.00

The Hardship Post
Jehanne Dubrow
ISBN 978-0977089260
$12.00

The Old Cities
Marcel Brouwers
ISBN 978-0972322492
$12.00

One Perfect Bird
Letitia Trent
ISBN 9780972322485
$12.00

Like a Fish
Daniel Crocker
ISBN 0-9723224-7-7
$12.00

The Bone Folders
T.A. Noonan
ISBN 978-0-9723224-6-1
$14.99

major characters in minor films
Kristy Bowen
ISBN 978-1939675194
$12.00

Exodus in X Minor
Fox Frazier-Foley
ISBN 978-1939675187
$10.00

CPSIA information can be obtained
at www.ICGtesting.com
Printed in the USA
FFOW02n1612130315
11736FF